GARY LIGHTBODY

Through the Storm: Gary Lightbody's Raw Journey of Pain, Passion, and Triumph

Table of Contents

Foreword 6

Introduction 10

Chapter One..15

    The Boy from Bangor 15

Chapter Two 20

    The Poet Finds His Voice 20

Chapter Three 26

    The Wild Years 26

Chapter Four...34

Beats, Basslines, and the Art of Reinvention..34

Chapter Five 43

    The Architect of Sound 43

Chapter Six..51

    The Architect of Soundscapes........................51

Chapter Seven 61

  The Alchemist of Emotion 61

Chapter Eight 70

  The Changing Tides of Sound 70

Chapter Nine 77

  Love, Loneliness, and the Weight of the World
  77

Chapter Ten 85

  Giving Back and the Power of Music 85

Chapter Eleven 97

  The Forest is the Path: A Journey into the Heart
  of Loss 97

Foreword

In a world where celebrity often obscures the truth, few have experienced a journey as genuine, haunting, and ultimately redemptive as Gary Lightbody's. In *Through the Storm: Gary Lightbody's Raw Journey of Pain, Passion, and Triumph*, we are invited into the life of the Snow Patrol frontman, delving into the heart of a man who has weathered intense challenges and emerged not just stronger, but also more authentic and deeply connected to the music that resonates with millions.

Gary Lightbody, the voice behind iconic songs like "Chasing Cars" and "Run," has lived a life that transcends the superficiality of fame. Each lyric and melody carries a narrative of struggle, a quest for purpose, and a confrontation with personal demons and loss. The untold stories—the late-night uncertainties, the internal battles, the love gained and lost, and the pains of growing up—are what truly define Gary as not only a musician but a genuine storyteller. This book invites readers into that world, offering a journey that is both heartbreaking and enlightening.

The public persona you may recognize—waking up to cheers in stadiums and living the rockstar lifestyle—belies a man who once faced financial struggles and questioned the worth of his efforts. Gary's ascent to success was marked by sacrifices, errors, and heartaches that many can only imagine. In *Through the Storm*, you will learn how the reflective moments in a small Northern Irish town evolved into powerful anthems that have become the soundtrack for countless lives.

This narrative goes beyond music; it explores the profound personal journey of a man unafraid to reveal his vulnerabilities, allowing his challenges and victories to infuse the melodies that have influenced a generation. However, this is not merely a tale of fame and success; it is a story of survival, rediscovery, and ultimately, redemption. Gary's journey was fraught with difficulties, including moments when it seemed he might lose the very gift that allowed him to connect through music.

As you read on, prepare to embark on a journey through loss, love, self-doubt, and eventual triumph. *Through the Storm* is not just about a musician; it is a testament to the resilience of the human spirit. It tells the story of a man who navigated through adversity, found his voice again, and in doing so, gifted us with songs that resonate in ways that words alone cannot capture.

Gary Lightbody is more than a pop culture icon; he is a source of inspiration for anyone who has faced challenges, questioned their self-worth, or emerged stronger from difficult times. His journey exemplifies how the toughest paths can lead to the most rewarding destinations.

This is more than just a biography; it serves as a tribute to resilience, the influence of music, and the passion that drives every lyric. Welcome to Gary Lightbody's authentic and unrefined journey. Welcome to Through the Storm.

Introduction

There are few narratives that possess the ability to engage, inspire, and remind us that the most significant victories often arise from profound challenges. Gary Lightbody's life is one such narrative—one marked by fervor, suffering, resilience, and ultimately, an unwavering success that has not only shaped him into the artist we recognize today but has also resonated with millions globally.

In *Through the Storm: Gary Lightbody's Raw Journey of Pain, Passion, and Triumph*, we delve into the life of a man whose journey was anything but straightforward, stepping beyond the glitz of fame. The world has experienced his voice, embraced his music, and joined in the anthems of hope, love, and loss that characterize Snow Patrol. Yet, behind each lyric and soaring chorus lies a narrative that is far more intricate than most realize.

Gary Lightbody's path to success was not lined with shining accolades or a life of ease. Instead, his journey was shaped by struggles—a constant tempest of doubt, heartbreak, and setbacks. Growing up in Northern Ireland, Gary aspired to be more than just a musician; he envisioned rising above his circumstances and achieving heights he had never dreamed of in his quiet, small-town upbringing. However, the road to fulfilling this dream was anything but smooth.

For years, he wrestled with self-doubt and the immense pressure to validate himself. He navigated through the darkness of personal and professional obstacles, when the future felt uncertain and every opportunity seemed to vanish as quickly as it appeared. There were moments when his own voice felt like a mere whisper amidst the chaos, a sentiment familiar to those pursuing their passions against the odds. Yet, through it all, Gary never abandoned his music—or his belief in himself.

This biography goes beyond simply chronicling the formation of one of the world's most cherished bands. It tells the story of a man who discovered comfort and purpose in the very thing that led to his greatest achievements: songwriting. It reflects a spirit that infused his pain into every note and lyric, allowing his struggles to lay the groundwork for the anthems we cherish today. In this way, Gary Lightbody evolved into not just a musician, but a symbol of hope for anyone who has faced rejection, uncertainty, or adversity.

As you read, you will be drawn into the most profound moments of vulnerability and victory. You will accompany Gary through his struggles with mental health, the heartbreaking loss of a loved one, the complexities of relationships, and the undeniable magic that emerges when a creative mind is pushed to the edge of both brilliance and madness. This is a journey that will challenge, inspire, and move you in ways you never anticipated.

Gary Lightbody often expresses that the best music originates from the most genuine and heartfelt places within us. His own story reflects this sentiment. "Through the Storm" is more than just a memoir of a man who became famous; it narrates the journey of someone who confronted challenges, embraced them, and emerged stronger, wiser, and more in touch with his true self than ever. With openness, sincerity, and a deep love for the music that helped him, Gary Lightbody's story will make you feel as though you not only understand the person behind the music but also share in the essence of his victory.

This narrative is not solely about achieving success; it's about survival. It's about discovering your voice when the world urges you to be quiet, about reclaiming your strength after everything has crumbled. It's about uncovering passion and purpose in the bleakest moments. Ultimately, it's about triumph—a victory not just for Gary, but for anyone who has ever dared to dream, hope, love, and rise from adversity.

Welcome to "Through the Storm." It's a journey through the pain, passion, and triumph that not only shapes Gary Lightbody's life but also encapsulates the human experience.

Chapter One

The Boy from Bangor

The rain pounded against the windows of the Lightbody residence in Bangor, County Down, as the Atlantic wind howled through the streets. This town, situated along Ireland's rugged northern coast, was accustomed to such storms, just as it was familiar with the gentle rhythm of daily life, occasionally interrupted by bursts of passion and song. However, within one particular home, a different kind of storm was brewing—not one of wind and rain, but of rhythm and melody, poised to be released.

Gareth John Lightbody entered this world on June 15, 1976, his cries blending with the timeless symphony of the Irish sea. To his parents, Lynne and Jack Lightbody, he was their pride and joy, a child embodying the same spark of independence and determination that flowed through their family. Jack, a businessman with deep connections to the historic city of Derry, had built his career from scratch, a quality that young Gary would unknowingly inherit in ways that were yet to be revealed.

From a young age, Gary was immersed in music—not through grand orchestras or sophisticated compositions, but through the everyday rhythms of life in Northern Ireland. The sounds of the marketplace, the laughter of his sister Sarah, and the distant strumming of guitars in smoky pubs all seeped into his subconscious. There was an intangible quality in the air—something beyond the constant scent of salt and rain—that suggested the extraordinary.

Yet, childhood was not solely filled with poetic inspiration. Bangor was a town steeped in history, shaped by the lingering effects of The Troubles, the conflict that marked Northern Ireland for decades. Even as a child, Gary recognized that music offered an escape, a powerful force that could transcend politics and turmoil, serving as a bridge between different worlds. While others resorted to violence, Gary would soon turn to a guitar.

However, his initial encounter with music was not love at first sight. In school, Gary was a dreamer, often lost in thoughts that wandered beyond the classroom, beyond Bangor, and even beyond Ireland. Teachers frequently urged him to "pay attention," but how could he when melodies danced in his mind like spirits, waiting to be released? His academic reports were filled with comments about his distracted focus, but his heart had already found its path.

Then came the moment of revelation. One day, in the cramped corner of a friend's house, he picked up a worn-out guitar. It wasn't a particularly impressive instrument—its strings buzzed, and its body was scratched—but when he strummed that first hesitant chord, something clicked. It wasn't merely a note; it was an opening, a whisper from destiny.

In the years that followed, Gary immersed himself in music with an unquenchable thirst. He became fixated on songwriting, jotting down lyrics in notebooks, on napkins, and even on the backs of school assignments. He soaked up influences like a sponge, from Leonard Cohen's introspective poetry to the powerful anthems of U2. There was no doubt about his purpose—only an intense desire to pursue it.

However, raw talent was not enough. The journey to fame was fraught with challenges, and before he could perform on international stages as the frontman of Snow Patrol, Gary would face setbacks, heartbreak, and moments of deep uncertainty. He would need to leave the familiar streets of Bangor and the comfort of home, venturing into the unknown with only his guitar and an unwavering faith in the power of music.

What he didn't yet understand was that the songs he had yet to create—the melodies still hidden within him—would one day resonate in stadiums, on the radio, and in the hearts of millions. The boy from Bangor was destined for something extraordinary. He just didn't realize it yet.

Chapter Two
The Poet Finds His Voice

The classroom was quiet except for the steady voice of the teacher at the front, reading from a worn book. The words drifted through the air like whispers of an ancient spell, enveloping the students, who listened with varying levels of engagement. Some fidgeted, eager for the bell to ring, but one boy remained completely still, captivated by every word.

Gary Lightbody had encountered countless words before—millions of them. He had read books, listened to discussions, and even penned his own stories. But this experience was different. This was Seamus Heaney, and the poet's lines resonated within him like a thunderous revelation. He wasn't merely hearing the words; he was experiencing them.

It was at Campbell College, following years at Rathmore Primary and Rockport School, that Gary's creative passion ignited. Heaney's poetry, rich with themes of land, history, love, and loss, was expressed in a language that was both simple and profound, shaking Gary to his very core. It felt as though the poet was reaching out from the pages, whispering to him that words were more than mere ink; they had the power to create worlds, shatter hearts, and save souls.

For the first time, Gary felt an intense urge to write—not just stories or essays, but something raw and personal, something that resonated like music even before it had a tune. Thus, he began to jot down his thoughts in the margins of his schoolbooks and on bits of paper. Initially, these were just lines, fragments of ideas that barely made sense. But as time went on, those lines evolved into verses, those verses into songs, forming the foundation of who he would eventually become. Yet, poetry alone would not define his identity.

A Leap into the Unknown

By 1994, Gary Lightbody found himself at a pivotal moment. Bangor had been his home for eighteen years, a place of comfort and familiarity. However, an inner restlessness—the same drive that had led him to music—urged him to leave. He felt the need to explore the world beyond Northern Ireland, to pursue something greater than himself.

Scotland beckoned.

With a blend of excitement and apprehension, Gary packed his belongings and headed to Dundee to study English Literature at university. The decision felt instinctive—words had become essential to him, and literature was the closest field to music he could pursue academically. But as soon as he stepped off the ferry onto Scottish land, he sensed something unsettling.

For the first time in his life, he found himself alone. University was an entirely new environment. The streets of Dundee felt foreign, filled with strangers speaking in unfamiliar accents. The university's expansive halls and lecture rooms resonated with the confident voices of students, which was both thrilling and intimidating.

Initially, he faced challenges. He longed for home, for the familiar streets of Bangor, the comforting sound of his mother's voice, and the ease of his previous life. However, Gary had learned from music that discomfort could often lead to the creation of the best songs. Instead of withdrawing into isolation, he immersed himself in the experience.

He participated in hockey, though it felt more like a duty than a passion. Saturday mornings often found him reluctantly pulled from bed by his teammates, grumbling and still half-asleep, yet he played anyway. It served as a distraction—a means of fitting in, even if his heart was elsewhere. Yet, his true passion was beginning to emerge in a way he didn't fully comprehend.

The Emergence of a Songwriter

Late at night, when Dundee was calm and his dormmates were asleep, Gary would sit in his small room with a notebook in front of him, his mind buzzing with ideas. He still cherished poetry, but it wasn't enough; he craved music and sought a way to transform his thoughts into something real.

Amid the chaos of student life, hockey matches, and literature classes, he picked up a guitar and began to play seriously. It became more than just chords and melodies; it was about discovering his voice. With each late-night strum and every lyric he wrote, he was drawing closer to that discovery.

However, music was still just a concept, a distant dream. Unbeknownst to him, his world was on the verge of transformation. Friendships would blossom, bands would emerge, and Gary Lightbody was about to embark on a journey that would lead him to something far greater than he had ever envisioned.

He was no longer merely a boy from Bangor; he was a poet, a dreamer, and a musician on the brink of something remarkable. And this was just the beginning.

Chapter Three

The Wild Years

The neon lights of Sauchiehall Street flickered on the wet pavement as Gary Lightbody emerged from Nice n Sleazy's, the air heavy with the smell of beer and cigarette smoke. He rubbed his hands on his jeans, feeling exhaustion seep into his bones. The bar job barely provided enough to get by, but it was a necessary burden—just another step on the ladder of survival in Glasgow's unforgiving music scene.

The city buzzed with sound—guitars being tuned in underground venues, voices rising in drunken song, and the distant thump of bass reverberating through club walls. It was chaotic, messy, and completely intoxicating. This was Glasgow, a city that had embraced him, knocked him down, and—slowly, almost unnoticed—begun to shape him into the musician he was destined to become. But nothing came easily.

The Birth of a Band

In 1994, Gary took his first significant step into the music world by forming a band with his university friend Mark McClelland and drummer Michael Morrison. They named themselves Shrug, reflecting their laid-back, almost reckless approach to their future. They weren't focused on fame or fortune—just on making music, writing songs, and seeing where it would take them.

Their early performances were rough. They played to half-filled bars, their songs receiving either polite applause or complete indifference. But their passion was undeniable and burned brightly. When Morrison eventually left the band, they had to change their name after discovering another group had already taken

Shrug. They rebranded as Polarbear—a name that initially felt like a fresh beginning.

With the addition of drummer Jonny Quinn, the band found a new rhythm, both literally and figuratively. They poured their hearts into their first two albums, *Songs for Polarbears* and *When It's All Over We Still Have to Clear Up*, recording in Glasgow and scraping together whatever resources they could. While the albums didn't achieve massive commercial success, they garnered a dedicated following and established the band as a formidable presence.

They toured tirelessly, sharing stages with bands like Levellers, Ash, and Travis. The road became their home—cramped tour vans, sticky hotel carpets, and countless late nights spent pursuing a fleeting dream. Glasgow remained their anchor, the place they returned to recharge, regroup, and plan their next steps. But for Gary, something was beginning to unravel.

Drowning in the Darkness

Music had always been his lifeline, but as the years went by and financial success remained frustratingly elusive, the pressure began to build. He felt trapped—caught in a cycle of near-successes and empty wallets. The band was surviving, but just barely. And in the quiet moments between gigs, when the adrenaline faded and reality set in, doubts crept in like shadows. So, he turned to drinking.

What began as a means of escape gradually turned into a routine. The drinks accumulated, late nights bled into early mornings, and the reflection in the mirror became unfamiliar. He described himself as "irrational, erratic, neurotic." Frustration escalated into rage, which he unleashed on stage.

He began to insult audiences, attacking the very fans who came to enjoy his music. He destroyed guitars that were beyond their budget to replace, the sound of splintering wood echoing through the venue like a desperate plea for help. His bandmates observed in silence, torn between loyalty and fear, uncertain of how to rescue him from his downward spiral.

For two years, this decline persisted. As success eluded them, Gary sank deeper. The path that once seemed full of potential now felt like an endless tunnel, devoid of light. He felt lost and directionless, convinced they were merely going in circles, doomed to fizzle out before ever truly igniting.

Then, a shift occurred.

The Turning Point

It wasn't a singular event, but rather a series of realizations—subtle truths that settled deep within him.

He looked at his bandmates, the ones who had remained by his side through his self-destruction. He noticed the weariness in their eyes, the burden of his turmoil weighing heavily on them. He recognized the remnants of the guitars he had broken, the destruction he had caused.

And he confronted himself—who he had become, what he was jeopardizing, and what he was on the verge of losing.

Gradually and with difficulty, he began to reclaim himself. He distanced himself from the brink, taking careful steps. He didn't completely stop drinking, but he learned to enjoy it rather than rely on it. He channeled his frustrations into music instead of alcohol, expressing himself through lyrics instead of chaos. His bandmates, who had stood by him through the turmoil, became his source of redemption.

The song "Disaster Button" from *A Hundred Million Suns* would later encapsulate that tumultuous time—a reminder of how close he had come to losing himself.

Discovering His Voice

Despite everything, one aspect stayed constant: Gary's voice. He couldn't read music—he confessed he just "guessed" his way through the chords—but his instincts were unmistakable. His rich baritone delivered his words with a profound impact. He didn't rely on sheet music or formal education; he possessed something far more valuable. He had emotion.

As he emerged from his most challenging years, something extraordinary awaited him.

A new identity. A fresh sound.

Snow Patrol was on the verge of taking off.

And this time, nothing would hold them back.

Chapter Four

Beats, Basslines, and the Art of Reinvention

The nights in Dundee were dominated by The Spaceship. The Tay Hotel thrummed with energy, its walls resonating with the fusion of house, rock, and hip-hop. Beneath the dim, flickering lights, students, artists, and musicians immersed themselves in the music, moving in unison and yielding to the rhythms. At the center of it all was a group of young men who were not merely playing music—they were crafting an experience. Among them, leaning over turntables with a cigarette hanging from his lips, was Gary Lightbody.

In the years leading up to Final Straw, before Chasing Cars transformed everything, and before Snow Patrol became a globally recognized name, Gary was a DJ, a poet, and a dreamer, spinning records in a makeshift club, with his future still unwritten.

The Birth of The Spaceship

Gary arrived in Dundee in 1994 as an English Literature student, but within months, he discovered something far more exhilarating than textbooks and lectures. He met Nick DeCosemo, a fellow student with an energetic spirit and a keen ear for music. The two quickly became close friends, united by their passion for sound, rhythm, and the electrifying power of a single track.

Before long, Gary moved out of his parents' home into his own apartment in Springfield. This marked a step toward independence—chaotic, unpredictable, and thrilling. With this change came The Spaceship.

Nick had initiated the club night at the Tay Hotel, which rapidly evolved into more than just another student gathering. It became a movement, a place where music collided in unexpected ways—house beats intertwining with rock riffs, hip-hop verses merging with electronic synths. It was a sonic rebellion, and Gary was right in the midst of it.

Alongside Nick, their group expanded to include Roy Kerr, Tom Simpson, and Anu Pillai—each contributing their unique influences, styles, and a shared desire for something different. They were not just DJs; they were creators of atmosphere, architects of unforgettable nights.

For two years, they dominated The Spaceship, cultivating a dedicated following. Music was their currency, their means of communication, their escape. Amidst it all, Gary was discovering his own rhythm—

not just as a DJ, but as a musician on a quest for his authentic sound.

The Hangover and the Hit

Yet, even as he played records into the early morning hours, Gary's own music was waiting for its moment. One night, nursing a hangover, he found himself at Anu Pillai's home. The two had been friends for years, and Anu—part of the electronic music group Freeform Five—was in the process of writing an album. He had a song, an idea, a hook that needed an extra touch.

Gary, on the other hand, was far from ready to be productive. His head throbbed, his body was sore, and all he desired was to sleep off the previous night's indulgences. However, Anu had different ideas. He physically pulled Gary to the studio, placing a pen and paper in front of him. Thus, amidst the haze of fatigue, "What Are You Waiting For" came to life.

The song, featured on Freeform Five's album "Strangest Things," marked a significant shift from Gary's previous work. It wasn't the guitar-driven indie rock he was known for; instead, it was sleek, vibrant electronica, an anthem for the dance floors he had often commanded. It demonstrated that his songwriting could transcend the realm of Snow Patrol, break through genre boundaries, and defy expectations.

At that moment, it was just another collaboration, another fleeting experience in the whirlwind of his early career. Yet, in hindsight, it represented something greater—a glimpse into the versatility that would come to characterize his future.

From DJ Booths to Radio Waves

As Snow Patrol's success began to unfold, Gary maintained his ties to the DJing scene. Even as the band gained popularity, he still carved out time to return to the decks, relishing the simple pleasure of mixing and creating new sounds.

In 2007, he found himself stepping into a different spotlight—this time as a guest host on BBC radio. DJ Zane Lowe, a highly regarded figure in music radio, was taking a break, and the BBC sought guest hosts to fill in. Gary was invited to take over for one night, a challenge he approached with both enthusiasm and a touch of anxiety.

Radio presented a different challenge. There was no audience to energize him, no dance floor to gauge, just a microphone and an unseen audience hanging on his every word. However, once the music began, it felt instinctive. He spoke, played tracks, and guided listeners through a set that was as varied and unpredictable as his own influences.

When the listener votes were tallied, it was clear: Gary Lightbody was their favorite among all the guest DJs.

The Late-Night Legacy

Gary's passion for DJing continued to flourish. He went on to create two mix albums, each showcasing his diverse musical tastes.

The first, "The Trip: Created by Snow Patrol," was part of the beloved Trip series, offering an immersive experience through the music that inspired him. It wasn't about chasing hits or following trends; it was about establishing a mood, a soundtrack for night owls, insomniacs, and wanderers.

The second, "Late Night Tales: Snow Patrol," was even more personal. The Late Night Tales series was renowned for featuring artists curating albums meant for the quiet hours when the world slowed down and the mind could wander. For Gary, this was a sacred opportunity. He and Tom Simpson poured their souls into the selection, crafting something that felt intimate and almost dreamlike.

This demonstrated that Gary Lightbody was more than merely a lead singer; he was a storyteller across various formats. Whether through his lyrics, DJ performances, or thoughtfully assembled mix albums, he possessed a natural talent for crafting memorable moments that lingered with people long after the music faded.

A Versatile Artist

As Snow Patrol rose to fame, Gary retained the lessons learned from The Spaceship. His eclectic style, unpredictability, and willingness to mix genres and challenge norms all contributed to the artist he evolved into.

Now, when he performs on stage with his band, and his voice resonates in stadiums filled with thousands, a part of him still recalls those nights in Dundee—the packed dance floors, the crackling vinyl, and the excitement of a perfectly timed beat drop. Gary Lightbody has never been defined by a single role. He is a poet, a rocker, a DJ, and a sound curator. Throughout it all, the music has never ceased.

Chapter Five

The Architect of Sound

The atmosphere was thick with the scents of whiskey and ink. Gary Lightbody was hunched over a notepad in the dimly lit corner of a Glasgow pub, surrounded by the soft murmur of strangers. He wasn't there to drink like he used to; he was there to write. Words had always been his sanctuary, a means to find clarity in the midst of chaos, and now they poured from his pen in a jumble of incomplete thoughts and fleeting melodies captured in ink.

This was no longer solely about Snow Patrol. His perspective had expanded, reaching far beyond the indie-rock anthems that had once defined him. He was no longer just a frontman; he had evolved into a collaborator, a writer, and a curator of music in all its forms. The world was beginning to acknowledge the depth of his influence.

A Soldier's Song

On a chilly, windswept set in Ireland, Gary adjusted his armor, feeling the weight of the chainmail on his shoulders. The air was thick with the smell of damp earth and burning torches. Extras and crew members rushed around him, preparing for another take. He wasn't there as a musician; he was portraying a Bolton soldier.

The opportunity had come unexpectedly. Game of Thrones, a cultural phenomenon, had reached out with an offer: a cameo in the episode "Walk of Punishment." The role was minor—a nameless soldier with a song to sing—but for Gary, it held significance.

As the cameras rolled, he began to sing:

"The bear, the bear, and the maiden fair…"

His voice resonated through the scene, haunting and melodic, filled with the same raw emotion that characterized Snow Patrol's music. In that moment, he wasn't just a musician; he was a storyteller in a different form, seamlessly blending his passion for words and melodies into a new realm.

It was a brief moment, an appearance that could easily be missed. Yet, it served as a reminder that Gary Lightbody was never meant to be limited to a single path.

The Writer's Soul

Throughout his songwriting journey, Gary had also been deeply passionate about writing about music itself. His love for music extended beyond performance; it was an obsession, a drive to explore, analyze, and share. He had always been a dedicated fan, and that commitment infused his writing. Over the years, he contributed essays, reviews, and recommendations to some of the most respected music publications.

As a guest editor for The Irish Times, he shared his musical influences with readers, introducing them to artists who had a profound impact on him. His articles transcended mere reviews; they were genuine tributes to the craft of songwriting and the albums that had been his companions during both tough and joyful moments.

At Q Magazine, he continued this philosophy, with his writing reflecting the same vividness as his lyrics. Whether he was dissecting a classic album or shining a light on an underrated artist, his prose conveyed the fervor of someone who truly immersed himself in music. He was more than just a musician; he was an advocate for the art form itself.

The Birth of The Reindeer Section: A Supergroup

One of his most notable acts of musical generosity took place in 2000. The indie-rock scene was bustling with talent, as bands collaborated, toured, and shared experiences in tight green rooms. Gary envisioned a unifying idea: What if they all came together?

He reached out to friends, bandmates, and anyone who shared his passion for melody and collaboration, leading to the creation of The Reindeer Section, a distinctive supergroup.

Forty-seven musicians from twenty different bands—including Belle & Sebastian, Mogwai, Idlewild, Teenage Fanclub, and Arab Strap—joined forces under one name. It was a chaotic, ambitious, and beautiful endeavor.

In 2001, they released *Y'All Get Scared Now, Ya Hear!*, an album that felt like a warm, drunken embrace among old friends. This was followed by *Son of Evil Reindeer* in 2002, which cemented their reputation as one of the most fascinating collaborative projects of the era.

For Gary, this was a confirmation of his long-standing belief: music is meant to be shared.

The Collaborator

As Snow Patrol's fame increased, Gary's desire to experiment with new sounds and engage in other projects grew stronger. In 2001, he lent his vocals to Mogwai's *Rock Action*, blending his voice with the Scottish post-rock band's ethereal style. That same year, he collaborated with British breakbeat artist Cut La Roc, diving into electronic beats and lively rhythms.

However, his most significant collaboration came in 2005. That year, The Cake Sale was formed—a collective of musicians coming together to support Ireland's Make Trade Fair campaign. Led by Brian Crosby of Bell X1, Gary enthusiastically accepted the invitation to join.

He collaborated with the enchanting Lisa Hannigan, providing vocals for the song "Some Surprise," written by Paul Noonan of Bell X1. The song gained traction, climbing the Irish charts and resonating with listeners on a deep level. It became more than just a song; it symbolized a movement, showcasing music's power to inspire change and promote goodness.

In 2006, he continued his artistic journey by contributing his voice to Freelance Hellraisers' album "Waiting for Clearance" and appearing on UK producer Kidda's debut album "Going Up." Each project was distinct, and every collaboration offered a fresh experience. Gary thrived on the unpredictability of it all.

The Ongoing Transformation

At this stage, it was clear that Gary Lightbody could not be limited to just one band, genre, or persona.

He was a frontman, DJ, songwriter for others, music journalist, curator, collaborator, and actor. Most importantly, he was a storyteller. Each song, article, and mix he produced added another piece to the puzzle—his life dedicated to music in all its varied forms. One thing was certain: Gary Lightbody was far from finished.

Chapter Six

The Architect of Soundscapes

The room was softly illuminated by a single studio lamp, creating a dim atmosphere. Gary Lightbody sat at the mixing desk, his fingers gliding over a notepad filled with partially completed lyrics. A quiet sense of anticipation hung in the air, a familiar vibe that always accompanied the start of something new and unexplored. He took a deep breath, reflecting on the past ten years—a whirlwind of transformation, collaboration, and unexpected developments.

For a long time, he had been recognized as the core of Snow Patrol, the voice behind anthems that had accompanied countless lives. But now, he was evolving into something entirely different—a composer, a collaborator, a creator of diverse sounds. And the world was paying attention.

The Song That Wouldn't Fade Away

It had begun as a gift.

Gary had penned "Just Say Yes" with Nicole Scherzinger in mind, intending it to launch her solo career. It was meant to be a pivotal moment, but fate intervened. Her album, *Her Name Is Nicole*, was put on hold, leaving the track in limbo. It nearly vanished into obscurity until The Pussycat Dolls tried to revive it. Yet, it still remained unreleased.

Some songs are not meant to be forgotten.

In 2009, as Snow Patrol prepared to release their compilation album *Up to Now*, Gary made a pivotal choice—"Just Say Yes" would finally be released. It would no longer belong to someone else; it would be his.

When the single debuted, it felt like poetic justice. It took off, captivating listeners with its vibrant energy and uplifting chorus. A song that had once been overlooked in the industry had finally found its rightful place.

It was more than just a song; it was a symbol of perseverance, ownership, and the belief that music has a way of finding its purpose, regardless of the challenges.

Creating a Legacy Beyond Snow Patrol

By this point, it was evident that Gary Lightbody was not limited to Snow Patrol. His creative aspirations reached far beyond the band that had brought him fame. In 2009, he took a significant step toward establishing that independence.

He announced two ambitious solo side projects:

- Tired Pony, a collective influenced by country and folk music.

- Listen… Tanks!, an avant-garde experimental project with Snow Patrol's producer, Jacknife Lee.

Tired Pony stood apart from the mainstream. It wasn't focused on creating stadium-filling anthems or the radio-friendly tunes typical of Snow Patrol. Instead, it was raw, poetic, and deeply human. While working on their debut album, *The Place We Ran From*, Gary found himself in Portland, Oregon, collaborating with a group of musicians who shared his artistic vision.

Among them were notable figures like Peter Buck, the iconic guitarist from R.E.M., Tom Smith from Editors, Richard Colburn from Belle & Sebastian, and many others. They weren't just producing an album; they were crafting something entirely new, a space where storytelling took precedence, echoing the spirit of classic country records.

Upon its release in July 2010, *The Place We Ran From* garnered attention. Critics hailed it as a significant shift, revealing a side of Gary Lightbody that few had witnessed before. It transcended mere polished hits; it was about creating atmosphere and depth, allowing the music to breathe.

Despite Tired Pony's success, Gary was eager to continue exploring new avenues.

That same year, he and Jacknife Lee composed the original score for the Irish film *My Brothers*, which debuted at the Tribeca Film Festival. This presented a fresh challenge for Gary, as he sought to convey emotion without lyrics, telling a story solely through sound. He relished the experience.

A Composer in the Making

Music evolved for him beyond just songs; it became about cinema and constructing entire worlds through sound.

This realization led to one of his most surprising collaborations: Ray Davies, the legendary former frontman of The Kinks. When Davies released *See My Friends*, an album featuring collaborations with prominent artists, Gary found himself recording "Tired of Waiting for You" with someone he had long admired. It felt surreal—a moment that completed a circle.

However, the most unexpected crossover occurred in 2012.

In Nashville, a young songwriter was finalizing an album that would transform her career. Her name was Taylor Swift, and the album was *Red*.

Having always been a fan of Snow Patrol, Taylor approached Gary about co-writing a song, and he eagerly accepted. Together, they created "The Last Time," a haunting orchestral duet that became one of the highlights of *Red*.

The collaboration felt destined—two songwriters known for their emotive storytelling joining forces at the perfect moment. Their performance of the song on *The X Factor UK* in 2013 was mesmerizing, their voices intertwining like old friends from another lifetime.

Years later, in 2021, Taylor Swift released *Red (Taylor's Version)*, a re-recording of the entire album that reignited interest in the song. Once again, "The Last Time" found its audience, illustrating how Gary's music has a unique way of lingering, waiting for the right moment to resurface.

The Visionary Behind the Curtain

By 2015, Gary had taken on a new role as a film composer. Together with his long-time collaborator Johnny McDaid, he was tasked with creating the score for *A Patch of Fog*, a chilling psychological thriller. Two years later, they collaborated again, this time for *Gifted*, a touching drama featuring Chris Evans.

This transition was subtle; while the public still recognized him as the lead singer of Snow Patrol, he was evolving into something greater: a sonic architect capable of infusing both lyrics and orchestral arrangements with deep emotion. This transformation extended beyond his own projects.

In 2009, he co-founded Polar Music, a publishing company aimed at supporting up-and-coming artists. Their first signing was Johnny McDaid, an underground songwriter who would later collaborate with Ed Sheeran, Alicia Keys, and P!nk. The company focused not just on discovering talent but on nurturing it, creating an environment where artists could flourish without being overwhelmed by the industry.

A Man of Many Sounds

By this point, Gary Lightbody's career had become multifaceted. He had penned chart-topping songs and film scores, formed supergroups, and performed duets with Taylor Swift. He had witnessed songs rise from obscurity and established platforms for new talent. Yet, amid all this, one undeniable fact remained: Gary Lightbody was still on a quest. He was in search of the perfect song, the next collaboration, and innovative ways to transform sound into emotion.

What lay ahead? Only time would reveal that. But history had shown one thing: Gary Lightbody was far from finished.

Chapter Seven

The Alchemist of Emotion

The attic room was small, hardly providing enough space for a teenager to stretch out. The air carried a faint scent of damp wood and old books, creating an atmosphere where secrets were held and stories were shared. In that cramped sanctuary beneath the family kitchen, Gary Lightbody sat with a guitar that was too large for him, his fingers awkwardly navigating chords he barely grasped.

He wasn't a musical genius. He had no formal training. In fact, he didn't even aspire to have any. What he truly desired was to experience something profound. So, at the age of fifteen, he began to write. Not because he believed he was talented, but because the words kept flowing.

They were raw, awkward, and incomplete—songs that he would later look back on with embarrassment. But they were his creations. In that tiny space, he could already feel it: the transformative power of music, the magic of turning emotions into sound.

He didn't need to master every chord; he just needed to understand himself. And that was sufficient.

The Influence of Music

Music was more than just something Gary listened to; it was something he absorbed deeply.

As a child, he was captivated by the rich arrangements of Quincy Jones and the infectious rhythms of Kool & the Gang. He danced to Michael Jackson long before he grasped the concept of rhythm. Then came Super

Furry Animals, a band that seemed to effortlessly defy conventions.

But when he hit his teenage years, guitars entered the picture.

Suddenly, his life was filled with the electrifying riffs of AC/DC and the dramatic flair of KISS. The raw, wild energy of hard rock was exhilarating, but it was alternative music that truly transformed him.

Bands like Pixies, Mudhoney, Sebadoh, and Pavement taught him that imperfection could be beautiful. They showed him that distortion and dissonance could be artistic. A song didn't need to be polished to hold meaning. These were the bands that inspired him to believe he could create music too. That he had to create music.

The Beauty of Simplicity

He wasn't initially a poet.

But discovering Seamus Heaney changed everything for him.

Heaney's writing had a unique ability to make the mundane seem remarkable. His poetry was straightforward yet impactful, prompting Gary to rethink everything he understood about writing. It wasn't about complexity or showing off; it was about authenticity. This realization became the cornerstone of his songwriting.

While other musicians played with complex metaphors and intricate wordplay, Gary opted for simplicity. His lyrics were straightforward, conversational, and candid. He believed that the most impactful songs felt like a chat with a friend—intimate, unfiltered, and genuine. This philosophy shaped the sound of Snow Patrol.

Tracks like "Run" and "Chasing Cars" were not technically intricate. They lacked elaborate progressions and unnecessary embellishments. Yet, they resonated deeply and universally, striking a chord with listeners. Gary understood that this emotional connection was crucial.

The Challenge of Love Songs

He never intended to focus on love in his writing. He wasn't aiming to be a hopeless romantic. However, love—and the pain associated with it—was a constant presence in his life. He drew from his own experiences, which taught him that love could be chaotic, flawed, and sometimes even disastrous. His songs were not fairy tales; they were honest confessions.

Take "Chocolate," for instance—a song born from guilt after he cheated on a girlfriend. It wasn't a passionate anthem; it was a quiet moment of reflection, a self-assessment set to music. This authenticity is what resonated with listeners. His music acknowledged that love isn't perfect, that it can hurt and sometimes fail. His songs captured the aftermath of grand declarations—the uncertainty, the regret, the yearning. They depicted real love in all its fragile imperfections. Even when he attempted to write about politics or broader issues, those songs felt forced and disconnected from his true voice. So, he stopped resisting and accepted that his music would always be deeply personal.

The Impact of His Words

It wasn't until 2009 that he realized how much his music had permeated the collective consciousness. At a party, a public figure—whose identity he never disclosed—pulled him aside and said, "You know, you've written standards." Gary was puzzled. "What do you mean?"

The person explained, "Your songs are now part of life. People sing them at weddings and funerals. They've become like the works of Frank Sinatra or The Beatles—songs that no longer belong to you; they belong to everyone." Gary was taken aback by this revelation.

He had never considered it that way before, but soon he began to notice it. People performing "Chasing Cars" on talent shows, choirs singing "Run," and strangers reaching out to him, sharing how his music had helped them through heartbreak, grief, and life's challenges.

It was a lot to take in. Yet, it was precisely the reason he had started writing in the first place—not to be trendy or to become a rock star, but to evoke emotions in others. Somewhere along the line, he had achieved that.

The Self-Effacing Genius

Despite his success and recognition, Gary Lightbody remained humble. He still felt embarrassed by his early work, considered his songwriting to be "basic," and often joked about being a "terrible" guitarist who never progressed beyond simple chords. But that was his unique charm.

Simplicity was not a flaw; it was a strength. It allowed listeners to connect with his songs, to see their own experiences reflected in the lyrics, and to hear their stories within the melodies. This connection was something that no level of technical skill could replicate.

Gary Lightbody had dedicated his life to finding the perfect song, striving to transform emotions into music.

He wasn't sure if he had achieved that yet, but he was certain of one thing: he would never stop searching.

Chapter Eight

The Changing Tides of Sound

Gary Lightbody had always viewed music as an emotional currency, a universal language that united people across different times and places. However, as the music industry continued to change, he began to question what happens when that currency loses its worth.

He had witnessed the transformation firsthand. In the past, people purchased music out of genuine affection. They cherished physical copies, admired the album artwork, and memorized the liner notes. Music was something tangible, an investment of sorts. But now?

It had become something to stream, a fleeting experience activated by a simple click. A song could rack up millions of streams yet yield almost nothing for the artist behind it.

Gary recognized that technology had revolutionized everything. Still, he couldn't shake the troubling question: if people could access any music for free at any time, why would they ever choose to pay for it? This dilemma posed a significant threat to the survival of emerging artists and made him reflect on whether Snow Patrol had merely been fortunate.

A Band Built on the Road

The early days of Snow Patrol were incredibly tough. They endured long hours in cramped vans, performing for audiences that barely paid attention. The pay was minimal, and every album sold felt like a hard-fought triumph. Yet, one undeniable fact remained—if someone owned a Snow Patrol album, it was because they had made a conscious choice to do so. They had discovered the band, purchased the album, and held onto it.

There were no illegal downloads or leaked tracks—just a genuine, direct connection between the artist and the audience. It was through relentless touring and hard work that Snow Patrol established something meaningful.

Gary believed that if the industry had been as it is now when they were starting out, their experience would have been vastly different.

Bands were not being compensated.

Albums were not being purchased.

Music had turned into mere background noise, rather than something people truly owned.

This reality frightened him.

The Myspace Effect

Gary had a complex relationship with technology.

On one hand, he recognized its potential to connect artists with their fans. On the other hand, he felt a sense of blame towards platforms like Myspace for the industry's current state. Myspace was the first to allow users to listen to entire albums for free, conditioning listeners to expect immediate access without payment. And now? Streaming services had taken that expectation and made it the standard.

He observed new bands pouring their passion into their music, only to earn mere fractions of a penny for each play. He witnessed their struggles as they attempted to transform their love for music into a career in an industry that seemed to make it nearly impossible. This left him concerned about the implications for the future.

If young artists couldn't sustain themselves financially, how long would they continue to pursue their dreams? How many potential icons had already given up before they even had a chance to be heard? Would a band like Snow Patrol have managed to survive if they were starting out today?

The Burden of Early Success

Yet, there was another thought that troubled him. What if Snow Patrol had achieved success sooner? What if they had bypassed the years of hardship? What if their initial albums had been immediate hits, thrusting them into fame before they were prepared for it? Would they have coped well with that sudden success, or would it have shattered them?

Gary had always believed that the difficult years—filled with rejection, failure, and uncertainty—were what allowed them to endure. If success had arrived too quickly, they might have taken it for granted and lost the drive that fueled them. The challenges they faced made them value every single achievement and equipped them to endure the inevitable downturns.

Music was not just about crafting songs; it was about persistence. It was about weathering the storms and finding a way to thrive in an ever-evolving industry.

He had seen bands rise and fall in an instant, artists who shone brightly for a brief moment before disappearing. Snow Patrol had outlasted them not due to luck, but because they had fought for their place. They had never taken their success for granted, and they never would.

An Uncertain Future

As Gary looked at the new wave of musicians, he felt a mix of emotions: hope and fear.

Hope, because music would always endure. As long as there were stories to share and hearts needing music to help them navigate life, artists would continue to create.

Fear, because the system was stacked against them. Without change, earning a living from music was becoming increasingly rare. He was uncertain about what the future would bring, but he was certain of one thing: whether in a packed arena or a small, dimly lit bar, music remained magical. And as long as that magic persisted, there would always be someone, somewhere, ready to fight for it.

Chapter Nine

Love, Loneliness, and the Weight of the World

For someone who had penned some of the most romantic songs of his time, it was a curious contradiction: Gary Lightbody struggled with relationships. At least, that's what he convinced himself.

He had dedicated years to crafting lyrics that expressed love in its most beautiful and heartbreaking forms. His words had brought tears at weddings, set the mood for late-night confessions, and echoed through headphones in dimly lit rooms where hearts yearned for something deeper.

Yet, in his own life, love always seemed just beyond his grasp.

The Man Who Composed Love Songs but Couldn't Find Love

It wasn't that he hadn't made an effort.

He had experienced relationships—some brief, others more significant—but none had endured. He held himself accountable for that.

He was rarely in one place for long.

His music had taken him around the globe, from packed stadiums to quiet hotel rooms in unfamiliar cities where he would wake up confused, momentarily forgetting his surroundings. Tour buses, airport lounges, backstage areas—his life was a whirlwind, and genuine love required stability. But Gary had never been stable.

He was aware of the irony. He had spent his life writing about love, yearning for it in his songs. But when it came to his own experiences, he didn't know how to grasp it.

He had been deeply in love before—more than once—but something always went awry. He would undermine it, or distance would make it unfeasible, or poor timing would ruin everything. Time and again, he found himself alone, with only his music for company.

Was it simpler to express love in a song than to experience it in reality?

The Escape of Fiction: A Comics Enthusiast at Heart

Perhaps that was why he had always been drawn to comics.

From the moment he picked up his first X-Men comic as a child, he was captivated. There was something compelling about those narratives—outsiders striving for acceptance, characters grappling with powers they never sought, seeking connection in a world that often failed to understand them.

And Wolverine?

Wolverine was his favorite. The brooding, solitary figure with a troubled past and a heart he struggled to navigate. The indestructible man who still felt pain more intensely than anyone else.

Over the years, Gary had accumulated stacks of comics, many of which he had never even opened. He liked the thought that they could someday become valuable collectibles, that they might hold significance in the future—a hidden retirement fund made of paper and ink. But if he were honest, it wasn't really about the collecting. It was about finding a sense of belonging.

Despite his fame, the adoring fans, and the gold records, there was always a part of him that felt like an outsider. He was the awkward teenager who struggled to find the right words, the man who penned love songs but couldn't maintain a relationship.

Perhaps that's why he turned to music. It was his superpower. And like all great powers, it came with its own costs.

The road was a lonely place, a lesson he learned through experience.

For years, he sought solace in the one constant that had always been lurking in the background: alcohol.

Initially, it was just a source of fun—a way to relax and quiet the inner critic that told him he wasn't enough. It helped drown out the doubts, loneliness, and heartache. But eventually, it transformed into something more destructive.

There was a time when he was unpredictable, when the pressures of Snow Patrol's challenges and his personal frustrations made him unrecognizable. He would drink excessively, lose control, and cause chaos. He became reckless, destroying guitars they couldn't afford to replace and pushing away those who cared for him.

Even after Snow Patrol found success, the drinking didn't cease; it merely evolved. It shifted from a source of anger to a means of numbness. The nights spent on tour, the silence after performances, the empty hotel rooms made it all too easy to pour another drink and escape.

However, by 2016, something changed. He grew weary of it all—tired of waking up with a foggy mind, tired of losing precious time, tired of using alcohol to fill the voids that music couldn't.

So he made a decision. Before Snow Patrol recorded *Wildness*, he stopped drinking entirely. There was no dramatic rockstar moment or rehab scandal making headlines—just a quiet choice. A choice to reconnect with his feelings, to be present, and to embrace stillness.

Gary Lightbody found himself caught between two worlds.

Between Ireland and Scotland, the places that influenced him. Between fiction and reality, the tales he crafted in his songs and the ones he found difficult to live out. Between fame and solitude, between the dazzling lights of the stage and the quiet loneliness that followed.

And perhaps most importantly, between love and loss.

His songs were always infused with a sense of yearning; that was an integral part of his identity. But perhaps, just perhaps, he was finally beginning to stop fleeing from what he truly desired.

Maybe he was prepared to be still.

Maybe he was ready to discover the love he had spent his entire life singing about.

Chapter Ten

Giving Back and the Power of Music

Gary Lightbody has always believed in music's ability to transform lives. It has been the foundation of his career—serving as an escape, a lifeline, and a connection between solitude and community. As his own journey progressed, he increasingly recognized the importance of giving back to the community that had supported him. The music that had rescued and inspired him now needed to help others.

A Champion for Northern Ireland's Music Scene

For many musicians, achieving success often means leaving their hometowns in search of greater recognition and fame. However, for Gary, Northern Ireland was not merely a backdrop; it was central to his story.

Growing up in Bangor, where the music scene was more about survival than achieving stardom, Gary understood the challenges young artists faced in establishing themselves. This issue resonated deeply with him, lingering long after he had experienced global tours and award ceremonies. Many bands were departing in search of larger opportunities, causing the vibrant energy of Northern Ireland's youth to fade from the limelight. That's when Gary felt compelled to make a change.

He became a passionate advocate for the burgeoning music scene in Belfast, promoting local talent and providing young musicians in Northern Ireland with a platform that had long been denied to them. As one of the few who had reached international success, his dedication to elevating the voices of the next generation became a key mission for him.

In 2009, during Snow Patrol's UK & Ireland Arena Tour, Gary made it a priority to give young Northern Irish bands the opportunity to open for them. This initiative was not about charity; it was about creating opportunities. Bands like Two Door Cinema Club, who were just starting to gain traction, shared the stage with Snow Patrol in front of thousands. This platform became a springboard for future stars, and Gary, in his own way, became a mentor to those who followed.

He often reflected on how significant it was for him to witness local heroes triumph against the odds while growing up. He aspired to be that hero for others.

The Lightbody Foundation: A New Chapter of Giving

The notion of giving back had always been on Gary's mind, but in 2019, he took a more structured approach. That summer, he established the Lightbody Foundation, a charity dedicated to causes he deeply cared about. Its mission was straightforward: to enhance lives through music, raise awareness of social issues, and support communities in need around the world.

At its heart, the foundation aimed to assist those who had supported him—musicians, young artists, and communities that often went unnoticed. He wanted to ensure that no one was left behind, especially in Northern Ireland, where the music scene had encountered its own challenges.

The foundation quickly emerged as a positive force. In May 2020, amidst the turmoil caused by the coronavirus pandemic, Gary promptly stepped up to help. He donated £50,000 to assist musicians in Northern Ireland who were struggling financially due to the closure of live music venues and the halt of the industry.

Gary's generosity extended beyond Northern Ireland as he reached out to the global community. Just two months after his initial donation, the Lightbody Foundation contributed $90,000 to nine different charities in the United States, all aimed at aiding individuals during the pandemic and providing relief to those in dire need.

The Lightbody Foundation: Advocating for Important Causes

However, the Lightbody Foundation was not solely focused on music; it aimed to create a meaningful impact in the world. Gary's dedication to supporting significant causes was profound. He had long been an advocate for Save the Children, an organization working to improve the futures of underprivileged children. In 2012, he embarked on a personal journey to Uganda, where he witnessed the harsh realities of poverty and violence affecting children. This experience profoundly changed him, and he wrote about it in the New Statesman, reflecting on the world's limited understanding of the severe human suffering in certain regions.

This trip further motivated him to take action. Gary realized that while he could change lives through music, he could also leverage his platform to amplify the stories that needed attention. He worked diligently with Save the Children and other charities to raise awareness for often-overlooked causes.

His commitment to raising awareness extended to mental health as well. Lightbody became an outspoken advocate, sharing his own struggles with depression. Music had served as a lifeline during his darkest times, and he wanted others to know they were not alone. He promoted discussions about mental health within the music community and beyond, aiming to dismantle the stigma that often kept people silent.

Recognition: Honoring a Legacy

It was evident that Gary's efforts had made a significant impact—not only in the music industry but also in the wider world. His charitable contributions, support for Northern Irish musicians, and relentless advocacy for those in need were duly recognized.

In 2012, the University of Ulster awarded him an Honorary Doctorate in Letters, acknowledging his remarkable contributions to music and his advocacy for important causes. This recognition was well-deserved for a man who had dedicated his career to not just entertaining, but also inspiring and uplifting others.

The accolades for Gary didn't end there. In 2018, he was awarded the Northern Ireland Music Prize in recognition of his significant contributions to music. This moment allowed for reflection on all he had contributed to the industry and his community, highlighting the journey from local performances to global recognition, and emphasizing the importance of remembering one's origins.

In 2020, his commitment to music and charitable work was further acknowledged when he was named an Officer of the Order of the British Empire (OBE) in the New Year Honours list. This was a significant milestone for someone who had dedicated his life not only to creating music but also to using it as a means to improve the world.

Then, in 2022, he received another prestigious honor—the Freedom of the Borough of Ards and North Down. This award celebrated his lifetime achievements and his commitment to his hometown and various causes, marking a proud moment for a man who always remembered his roots.

A Legacy of Generosity, Music, and Impact

Gary Lightbody understood the transformative power of music. It had provided him with purpose, fame, connections, and love. However, it was his realization that music alone was insufficient that truly shaped his legacy.

Through the Lightbody Foundation, he demonstrated his commitment to supporting young musicians, promoting mental health awareness, and championing charitable initiatives, evolving beyond just a rock star into a source of hope for those in need.

As the world around him changed, Gary remained dedicated to helping others. Whether through music, charity, or personal advocacy, he recognized that his true purpose was in giving back. In doing so, he created a legacy that would endure for future generations. For Gary Lightbody, music was merely the starting point.

Gary Lightbody's career has traversed various continents and musical styles, highlighting the emotional depth of his songwriting and the worldwide impact of his band, Snow Patrol. However, beneath the accolades and success, there has always been a more personal struggle, a deeper issue that has lingered. This underlying theme has been present in every album, lyric, and chord—a mystery he has yet to fully unravel. In his new book, *The Forest is the Path: A Special Companion to the Number 1 Bestselling Album by Snow Patrol*, Gary finally confronts the darker aspects of his life, offering readers an honest and unfiltered look into the experiences that shaped one of Snow Patrol's most significant albums.

The Numbness and the Pain

The book begins with the feeling of falling, a sensation Gary is intimately familiar with, both in a metaphorical and literal sense. For years, he felt as if he were plummeting through time, losing his connection to the world around him. When his father, Jack, died, that sense of disconnection intensified, and the world seemed to collapse entirely.

"You're falling through time so all I can do is fall with you," the opening line draws readers into the book's emotional terrain. The numbness that had gradually seeped into Gary's life culminates in this moment. As the plane lands in Belfast City, he describes a feeling that burns deeply within him. It's a striking and unsettling image—a man facing the heavy burden of time, loss, and the challenge of truly comprehending the gravity of his situation. While his senses may be dulled, the emotions remain, leaving an enduring mark.

This theme resonates throughout the book: time, loss, love, and the unavoidable reality of death. However, it is not merely a narrative of grief. Instead, it focuses on the journey itself, emphasizing the acceptance that life continues despite pain, and how the numbness that accompanies loss is also a part of the healing process.

Chapter Eleven

The Forest is the Path: A Journey into the Heart of Loss

The Prequel to the Album: The Heart of The Forest is the Path

While the book serves as a companion to Snow Patrol's album The Forest is the Path, it also functions as a prequel—an intimate look into Gary's personal journey that inspired the album's creation. Throughout the book, lyrics from the album are interspersed, guiding readers through the narrative of his father's death and the emotional turmoil that followed. The blend of song lyrics and prose offers a distinctive experience that reflects the dual aspects of Gary's creative process. While the music provides the soundtrack, the book offers the context—the story behind the sound.

For Gary, the numbness of loss was not a fixed emotion. It was a journey that, as he reveals in the book, awakened a previously dormant part of him. Following his father's passing, songwriting became his form of therapy, a means of processing grief and finding meaning amid chaos. Resuming songwriting after a period of emotional paralysis was not merely a healing process; it felt like a rebirth. It was as if a door had swung open, unleashing a torrent of ideas, emotions, and, most importantly, a renewed connection to life. Once again, the songs became his way of achieving balance in an unbalanced world.

Themes of Time, Home, and Love

The Forest is the Path boldly tackles complex themes, embracing them fully despite the emotional challenges they may present. Time, love, and home are recurring themes throughout the book, each explored with the raw honesty that characterizes Gary's songwriting. The loss of his father compels him to reflect on his own perception of time, particularly how it shifts in the face of death. Time transforms from something to be managed into something to endure.

Gary's connection to home is another key theme. Belfast and Northern Ireland have significantly influenced his identity, both personally and musically. However, while he yearns to return to Belfast, he also grapples with its complexities. The Forest is the Path reveals his mixed feelings about his roots. He acknowledges the comfort and solace his hometown offers, yet he also experiences a sense of isolation, a desire to escape the past while confronting it. The book captures the delicate balance between the urge to move forward and the undeniable pull of history.

Ultimately, it is love—along with its joys and complexities—that shapes the narrative of The Forest is the Path. Gary's struggles with love, relationships, and the people who enter and exit his life form the foundation of the book. At its core, his journey is a quest for connection—a search for understanding in a world that often feels bewildering.

The Purpose: A Message of Hope and Renewal

One of the most compelling elements of *The Forest is the Path* is how Gary guides his readers through a journey of emotional change. It starts in a place of deep sorrow but never remains there. There is a persistent sense of hope, a belief that even in the bleakest times, a light can lead you forward. The numbness that once engulfed him eventually transforms into a renewed sense of purpose. His father's death, though painful, becomes a turning point for personal growth—an awakening that profoundly impacts his life and music.

Gary emphasizes that this is not a book focused on perpetual mourning. Instead, it explores the journey of coming to terms with loss, highlighting that grief is not something to be defeated but rather understood and accepted. Through this understanding, a new strength arises—a strength that empowers him to continue creating, writing, and living.

A Companion for the Soul

The Forest is the Path is not just for Snow Patrol fans; it resonates with anyone who has faced loss, struggled with time, or sought direction in life. It addresses the human experience of confronting our mortality and the healing power of art.

As Gary notes, "You don't have to read this book to understand the album, but you may want to give it a wee listen for some parts of the book to make sense." The album and the book are closely linked, yet each can stand alone, contributing to a larger narrative. Together, they create a powerful message about life, love, and navigating the darkest moments of our journeys.

The book's release on March 13th represents a significant milestone in Gary Lightbody's career—not only as a musician but also as a storyteller who has learned to channel his pain into something beautiful through his art. In doing so, he offers us something truly extraordinary: a guide on how to confront loss, embrace the passage of time, and rediscover ourselves when the world feels overwhelming.

Printed in Great Britain
by Amazon

e361bbe5-45fc-442b-95f6-8b625f7b9885R01